Original title:
The Pomegranate's Heart

Copyright © 2025 Creative Arts Management OÜ
All rights reserved.

Author: Elliot Harrison
ISBN HARDBACK: 978-1-80586-328-1
ISBN PAPERBACK: 978-1-80586-800-2

Fragments of Forbidden Love

In gardens ripe, where secrets play,
Two lovers met by a fruit display.
She whispered sweet, he laughed out loud,
Their blushes crimson, so brightly proud.

With every bite, they shared a taste,
Juicy stains, their secret chased.
The seeds like giggles, bursting free,
Love's odd banquet, just you and me.

Tales Stained in Scarlet

In kitchens hot, a mishap grew,
A splash of red, and oh, what a stew!
Grandma's recipe, a slippery plight,
What once was dinner, now a fright!

With every spill, the laughter rose,
A playful dance, as chaos goes.
Tangled aprons, love's cheeky joke,
The mess was grand, but nobody choked.

The Lure of Liquid Gem

A goblet gleams, with ruby hue,
A twist of fate, and laughter too.
Sipping sweet nectar, joy takes flight,
Giggling shadows dance in the night.

Friends raise their cups, with glee anew,
"More for me, less for you!"
In this enchanted, tart embrace,
Joy spills over, a messy race.

Harvesting the Soul

On the farm, a playful raid,
Finding gems beneath the shade.
With baskets full and hearts so bold,
Stories of mischief, delightfully told.

As laughter rings through sunlight beams,
They dance like kids, lost in dreams.
The harvest was sweet, but what a fuss,
With juice-stained hands, they made a mess!

Seeds Beneath the Surface

Beneath my skin, they wiggle and squirm,
Hiding in chambers, oh what a term!
Each one is a surprise, a cheeky retreat,
I'm just a banquet of bites, isn't that neat?

When guests arrive, they can't quite believe,
I'm the fruity magician that they won't conceive!
With a pop and a crunch, they're caught off their guard,
A fruity explosion, it's never too hard!

The Burden of Red Flesh

Oh, this red coat, it's quite the display,
Too much drama for just a buffet!
Heavy with sweetness, but look at my seed,
They're the real show, and they always succeed!

People come over, they gawk and they stare,
What's your secret? They ask, with a flair.
I laugh and I wink, it's all in the skin,
When your heart's full of juice, let the fun begin!

Where Bitter Meets Sweet

In the dance of flavors, I twirl so spry,
A tangy tango that makes people sigh!
Sweet like a joke, but with a twist of the tongue,
Join the party, where the laughter is young!

"Is it a fruit or a riddle?" they say,
With a frown on their brows, come join in the play!
I'm the life of the feast; a comic delight,
Who knew fruit could be such a laugh in the night?

Harvest of Ancient Dreams

Plucking these jewels from branches above,
Whispers of secrets, and a pinch of love!
Ancient tales hidden in every bright sphere,
I giggle at history, oh dear, oh dear!

They say knowledge is sweet, but have you tried me?
In every red bite, there's a mischief spree!
So gather around for this curious feast,
A laugh in each layer, I can't be the least!

Kernels of Wisdom

In the orchard tall and grand,
Laughter spills like grains of sand.
Each kernel chuckles, oh so bright,
Tickling tongues with sheer delight.

Peel away the outer shell,
Inside jokes are hard to quell.
With a burst, they share a tale,
Of mischief brewed in summer's gale.

Come gather round, don't miss the fun,
A fruity feast for everyone.
With wise cracks popping left and right,
These kernels keep the mood just right.

Bright Hues of Heartbreak

Crimson stains on old white shirts,
Love's adventure with its quirks.
Splashed on fabric from a bite,
Who knew romance could cause such fright?

Each juice drop tells a ghostly story,
Of love's sweet and sour glory.
When hearts collide and squish so good,
It's chaos wrapped in nature's hood.

With giggles through this messy art,
We wear our scars, we play our part.
In every splash, a memory's made,
A blend of colors that won't fade.

An Offering from the Tree

A gift bestowed from leafy heights,
With winks and giggles as its sights.
Hunched over, looking for a prize,
A surprise within, oh what a guise!

The tree whispers, "Come take a peek,"
This treasure hides a fruity cheek.
A burst of flavor, oh what a treat,
Who knew a fruit could be so neat?

With sticky fingers reaching high,
We munch and laugh, oh my, oh my!
This offering's a jovial show,
A sweet reunion, don't you know?

The Dance of the Juicy Seed

A seed hops here and bounces there,
In the sun with joyous flare.
Round and round, it twirls with glee,
Begging everyone to join in free.

Chasing shadows, skipping heat,
Each juicy dance is quite the feat.
With krump and shuffle, what a sight,
Making pulses race with delight.

If you feel down, just take a spin,
Let laughter's rhythm pull you in.
For in this zest and happy beat,
Life's a party, oh so sweet!

Juices of Memory Linger

In the orchard where I play,
I tugged a fruit, it slipped away.
With juice that squirted, oh what a sight,
Red stains and giggles, such pure delight!

Each seed a story, a splash on my shoe,
I chased my dreams like I chased that dew.
A burst of laughter, a sweet little prank,
In sticky fingers, my spirit sank.

Grandpa warns me of juice that stains,
But how can I care when joy remains?
The memories linger, like seeds in a bowl,
Like tiny treasure, they fill up my soul.

A Garden's Hidden Pulse

In a patch where colors gleam,
I found a fruit that made me scream!
Not grapes or apples, it was bright,
A ruby gem that stole my sight.

The squirrels dance with little feet,
As I plot how they'll take my treat.
In secret gardens, mischief thrives,
With fruity jokes, this garden jives!

We laugh together, nature's crew,
The funny sights that we pursue.
With every bite, we flip and twirl,
This garden's pulse gives joy a whirl.

Sweetness and Sorrow Entwined

A fruit so bright, it sings a song,
Yet with each bite, you can't help but long.
The sweet and tart play hide and seek,
A giggle and sigh, they tease the week.

In every burst, a giggling tear,
It's joy and sadness that draw us near.
Whispers of flavor, a quirky twist,
In every crunch, you can't resist!

With friends around, we share our tales,
Mixed emotions on the scales.
A funny dance under the sun,
Where sweetness and sorrow become one!

Echoes of the Ruby Fruit

In the quiet shade, a secret hum,
The ruby calls me, come, come, come!
With dancing seeds and laughter near,
I tip my hat to the joyful cheer.

Each bite a burst, a funny sound,
As juice flies up and hits the ground.
With giggles echoing in the air,
The glorious mess we gladly share!

I'll wear the stains like a badge of pride,
The fruity laughter, oh, how it glides!
In moments sweet, we find our way,
With echoes of joy, we play all day.

Nectar's Embrace

In a garden, fruits do dance,
With rosy cheeks, they take a chance.
Juicy kisses, dripping sweet,
A fruity laugh, a tasty treat.

Sticky fingers, a giggling crew,
Sipping juice like it's taboo.
Each drop a joy, an acrobatic feat,
A one-man show on a trampoline seat.

Seeds like confetti, all around,
Pop them open, what a sound!
Laughter bubbles, echoing cheer,
Fruit fiesta, let's all draw near.

In the sun, we sing and sway,
Life's a joke, come join the play.
Nature's gifts, a silly game,
In each bite, a burst of fame.

The Weight of Sweetness

There's a fruit that weighs a ton,
Each bite feels like a loaded gun.
Sweetness drips, a sugar bomb,
One slice and you might go 'WHOM!'

Balancing acts on kitchen floors,
Slippery joys behind closed doors.
Wobbling plates, a feast of glee,
Watch your step, just wait and see.

Juicy treasures, that burst and pop,
Eating these, you'll never stop.
With every slice, your smile's wide,
A clowning show, you cannot hide.

Sweetness oozes, a funny sight,
Laughter bubbles, pure delight!
Can't contain, it's pure romance,
When food turns into a dance.

An Elixir of Hope

From the fruit, a potion spills,
Tasting joy, it brings you thrills.
With a giggle and a sip,
Life's a carnival, enjoy the trip.

A splash of red, a twist of rhyme,
Sipping nectar, passing time.
Each gulp's a joke, a wink, a grin,
Like a daredevil, where to begin?

Magical essence in every drop,
Hop on board, go make it pop!
Through laughter, we find our cheer,
This sweet elixir, let's all volunteer.

Bouncing joy on a silly ride,
Pouring smiles and nowhere to hide.
A sip of joy, a giggly fling,
Life's elixir makes us sing.

The Colors of Desire

In hues of red, we paint the day,
Color those dreams, come what may!
A splash of mischief, a dash of fun,
Fruitful laughter, a race begun.

Colors burst like fireworks bright,
Eating joy, what a delight!
Each shade a giggle, a twist of fate,
Paint the world, don't hesitate.

Cardinal shades in a bright parade,
Sweetened whispers, a daring escapade.
With every hue, a chuckle grows,
In this canvas, humor flows.

Join the feast, let's mix it up,
A vibrant world, join the cup!
Palette fun, in every bite,
Colors dance, pure delight!

The Alchemy of Taste

In a bowl so bright and round,
Where juicy gems can be found,
I ponder deeply, spoon in hand,
Why do they stain like a rebel band?

I took a bite, a burst of cheer,
My shirt now sports a crimson smear,
It's magic at play, a tasty jest,
An adventure for my taste buds' quest!

Each seed a treasure, they dance and sway,
A cheeky fruit in a grand buffet,
I laugh as red drips from my chin,
In the kingdom of snacks, it's a win-win!

So here's to the fruity, messy delight,
With every bite, I'm taking flight,
Who needs a napkin, I shout with glee,
This juicy chaos is just for me!

Delicate Darkness

In the shadow of sweet indulgence,
Darkness lurks with a mischievous stance,
A fruit so bright, yet seeds in disguise,
Whispering tales, oh what a surprise!

I hold it up, like a gem from a throne,
Timing my nibble—should I munch or moan?
The juice squirts out like a jester's joke,
Sticky fingers, and I start to choke!

The seeds roll wild, a comedic scene,
Like confetti at a messy cuisine,
I dive right in, splatter and all,
Who knew fruit could be such a brawl?

Giggling and munching, I can't take a break,
For laughter and juiciness are hard to shake,
In this tangle of fun, I have to agree,
Being messy is where I'm meant to be!

Mosaic of Memories

Bits of red scatter in my bowl,
Each shiny piece a joyful goal,
Memory triggers, sweet and grand,
Of all the times I couldn't stand!

I crack a seed, it hops and rolls,
A fruit parade, it jives and trolls,
With every pop, a giggle escapes,
As I juggle the bits like fruity grapes!

Oh, the laughter as they scatter far,
Like runaway marbles, how bizarre!
It's a mosaic of flavor, a crunchy mess,
With every bite, pure happiness!

In the midst of this fruity disgrace,
I wear the remnants like a badge of grace,
Laughter echoes, joy in my stride,
A dance of memories at snack time's side!

An Ode to the Scarlet Seeds

Oh, little rubies, bouncing high,
Your tartness echoes like a cheeky sigh,
In a bowl they gather, bright and bold,
A treasure trove of laughter to behold!

With each delightful pop, I decree,
You're the jester of my pantry, oh so free,
Like fireworks bursting under the sun,
What could be better than silly fruit fun?

I toss them up, in a sprightly dance,
Catching droplets, oh what a chance,
To wear the crimson like a badge of honor,
Messy and joyful, I'm the fruit bonner!

An ode to you, my ruby-red friends,
May the giggles and flavors never end,
In the theatre of snacks, you play your part,
With goofy delight, you steal my heart!

Heartbeats of Autumn's Sonnet

In autumn's chill, a dance begun,
With leaves that twirl and laughter spun.
A fruit so bold, with seeds that wink,
A juicy jest, more fun than drink.

The branches shake with playful glee,
While squirrels plot their next great spree.
They scheme to steal what's bright and red,
But I just grin and shake my head.

Each seed, a mystery, life's sweet game,
In nature's theater, none the same.
The crunch, the pop, each tasty bit,
Leaves gardeners in a giggling fit.

A harvest ripe, with laughter's tone,
Who knew a fruit could feel like home?
These heartbeats echo, warm and loud,
A frolicsome joy, we laugh, we crowd.

Serpents Among the Seeds

Among the seeds, a tale unfolds,
Some sly little snakes, oh so bold.
They wiggle in, with cheeky grins,
Claiming the fruit, oh where to begin?

With hearts so bright and laughter's cheer,
The garden sways, the snakes appear.
"Stop right there!" the fruit shouts loud,
"Not on my watch, you sneaky crowd!"

One serpent slips, a seed will pop,
Spraying juice, a messy drop.
The fruits unite, and so they jest,
"Join us now, forget the rest!"

In this wild game of chase and tease,
They share the laughs, a sweet unease.
For who can resist, when life's a feast,
With serpents, seeds, and joy increased?

The Allure of the Juicy Interior

Oh, juicy treasure, bright and bold,
Your charm it seems will never grow old.
With gleaming seeds, like tiny gems,
You dance on tongues like playful hymns.

Each bite a laugh, a burst of fun,
A playful prank from nature's gun.
"More, more!" we cry, as juice does fly,
In sticky joy, we cheer and sigh.

Your crimson hue is quite a lure,
With every taste, we want more, for sure.
In kitchens bright, the laughter rings,
As recipes are born from silly things.

A humor sweet, in every slice,
From silly spills to juicy spice.
Oh dazzling fruit, with hearts so pure,
You keep our spirits light and sure.

Sorrows in Scarlet Gowns

In gowns of red, the sorrows twirl,
Around the boughs, they spin and swirl.
Yet with each tear, a giggle's trace,
For even grief can find its place.

These fruits of sorrow, sweet and strange,
Bring laughter's light amidst the change.
With every bite, the memories dance,
Turning heartaches into chance.

A wink, a pop, in crimson glow,
We laugh at how life can overflow.
The juice runs wild, like tales retold,
Where laughter lives, though sorrows bold.

So gather round, don't let them frown,
In juicy friends, wear laughter's crown.
For in each heart lies fun to spare,
Even in gowns that once wore despair.

Beneath the Skins of Passion

In gardens bright, a secret lurks,
With juicy seeds that make me smirk.
Each bite's a pop, like gossip spread,
A splash of juice, and laughter's bred.

They blush and shine in ruby hues,
Like tipsy friends in crazy shoes.
I nibble slow, my fingers stained,
In sticky fun, no shame's retained.

Underneath this playful skin,
The wildest flavors spin and spin.
I munch and snicker, what a treat,
A feast that's subtly bittersweet.

If only fruit could tell a tale,
Of little hearts behind the veil.
With every crunch, a joke unfolds,
Sweet laughter wrapped in crimson folds.

Veins of Fruitful Regret

In glossy shells, my dreams reside,
Yet bites of truth are hard to hide.
Each seed a wish, some come in pairs,
For every joy, there's life that bears.

I tried to savor every drip,
But laughter's end came with a slip.
Regrets like juice upon my cheek,
A fruity mess that's oh so sleek.

These crimson globes, they tease and taunt,
With every munch, I fall and flaunt.
My taste buds dance, they twist and sigh,
Yet deep inside, I can't deny.

For fruit is fickle, sweet but sly,
It's hard to say goodbye, oh my!
Still, in this game of juicy fun,
I'll take the regret, it weighs a ton.

A Symphony of Arils

A crunch, a pop, a juicy fight,
Each tiny bit bursts pure delight.
With every seed, a note we find,
Creating chaos sweet and blind.

In rhythmic spoons, we gather round,
As laughter's chorus fills the sound.
Beneath the skins, a song's devised,
Of fruity whims and joys disguised.

Their ruby tunes weave tales of cheer,
With every squirt, the fun draws near.
A jester's feast, a banquet's jest,
No better way to spend a jest.

Yet watch your shirt, for drips abound,
An artful splash, a canvas found.
With every giggle, life's alive,
In this mad dance, we thrive and strive.

Nature's Intimate Offering

Oh nature's gift, you've done me well,
With seeds of joy that burst and swell.
These crimson treasures, how they gleam,
A playful prank, a juicy dream.

Each time I crack, a laugh erupts,
Like little jokes from nature's cups.
The juice takes flight, like laughter flows,
Splatters of fun where mischief grows.

With every scoop, surprises hide,
Like friends who sneak in for a ride.
Peeling back skins, I find a thrill,
With every taste, my heart does fill.

So here's to fruits, with wit and charm,
In every bite, they weave a balm.
Nature's offering, wild and free,
A joyful dance, just you and me.

The Architecture of Sweetness

In the garden, colors clash,
A fruit that makes the neighbors crash.
With seeds like jewels, oh what a sight,
I'll take a bite, and then take flight!

The juice drips down like a red parade,
Sticky fingers, oh I'm dismayed!
My shirt's now a canvas, quite a mess,
But who knew eating could cause such stress?

Each burst of flavor, sweet and strange,
My taste buds dance, quite out of range.
Biting too hard, then flinging seeds,
Oops! There goes one; my friend now bleeds!

Architecture of sweetness, it's a thrill,
Creating chaos, and there's more still!
The laughter echoes, we're all in stitches,
In the sweetest sport, we're the top pitches!

Biting into Memory

I chomped down hard, oh what a crunch,
It sent me back to childhood's brunch.
A sticky mess, the scent so bold,
Mom laughing at the tales retold.

Seeds flew wildly, like ninja stars,
My cousin ducked, said, "Watch those cars!"
With every bite, a story spins,
Jumping over gossip, snickering grins!

Juicy treasures spilling on the grass,
What's that stain? Oh, don't let it pass!
It's not a problem, just a classic,
When life gives mess, you get fantastic!

Memories coated in sugar and fun,
In this game of bites, we've already won.
Let's savor laughter, not just the taste,
Biting into joy, let's not waste!

Nectar and Nostalgia

The nectar flows like a river divine,
With laughter swirling, oh it's sublime.
What's that? A face? Were you caught?
In this sweet dance, who's really thought?

Tasting the past, oh honey and zest,
Each little seed feels like a jest.
Bouncing between flavors, a comedic spree,
Our giggles echoing, as sweet as can be!

A funny slip, and down I go,
With juice on my chin, I steal the show!
Cheeks full of treasures, can't talk at all,
But laughter erupts, it's quite a ball!

Nostalgia kinda thick, like syrupy glue,
With every bite, memories renew.
So we share a toast, with fruits all around,
In this sweet battle, hilarity's found!

Unraveling Sweetness

Crack that skin, watch the juice fly,
A splash of chaos, oh me, oh my!
Seeds like confetti, who threw that?
A sticky situation, where's my hat?

With every nibble, the laughter swells,
A fruit explosion, oh it tells.
Twirling like dancers upon the beat,
Who knew sweetness could be this sweet?

Unraveling layers, a sugary mess,
With every bite, I wear my dress.
Clothes are donning the red of delight,
Fashion advice? Avoid a fruit fight!

So here we are, in sweetness we trust,
A hilarity shared, that's a must.
With ridiculous memories, let's raise a cheer,
For fruits in our lives, and laughter near!

Love Wrapped in Red Skin

In a garden where laughter blooms,
The fruit with a wink breaks all gloom.
Red and round, oh what a sight,
Rolling around, it's out for a bite.

With seeds that pop like tiny balloons,
It dances in bowls, hums merry tunes.
A kiss from the sun, a joke from the tree,
Who knew love could giggle so cheekily?

It teases with tartness, then sweetly yields,
Making us grin while munching our meals.
The juice dribbles down in a playful fight,
We laugh at our faces—oh what pure delight!

In kitchens, it reigns, a jester in red,
With flavors that tangle, playfully spread.
To share it with friends is a double delight,
For nothing feels better than laughing outright.

The Ritual of the Harvest

Gather around, it's that time of year,
With baskets in hand, we'll conquer our fear.
Climbing the trees, we leap and we dive,
In pursuit of the treasure, we come alive.

The fruit that's so plump, it tugs at my sleeve,
"Pick me, oh pick me!" it laughs with reprieve.
We pluck and we giggle, our hair in a mess,
The bounty rewards us—oh, what a success!

With stains on our fingers, we dance on the ground,
Each bite is a riddle, a joke that's profound.
The neighbors look on, with envy they stare,
As laughter erupts—oh, sweet juicy fare!

At dusk, we sit back, our mission complete,
Sharing the stories of the day's wild feat.
While seeds fly like confetti in joyous embrace,
We wrap it all up with fruit juice on our face!

Tales of Transmutation

Once a simple seed, dreaming to grow,
Now a talkative fruit, putting on a show.
Whispering secrets in blossoms so bright,
A comic transformation, pure delight!

Wiggling and jiggling, it chuckles with glee,
"I'm not just a snack, I'm a party!" says he.
In the bowl, it spins, a vibrant red twirl,
Transforming a meal, who knew it could whirl?

Its seeds are confetti, bursting with cheer,
Each nibble brings giggles, banishes fear.
From dull to divine, it struts with such flair,
Life's a bowl of laughs, come join if you dare!

So when you partake of this fruity delight,
Remember the journey from seed to the bite.
A laugh and a crunch, together we'll sing,
In this kingdom of flavor, oh, what joy it brings!

Echoes of Sweet Yearnings

In dreams of sweetness, I often behold,
A fruit with a laugh, a story retold.
It sings to my soul, with bubbles of fun,
Each bite is a journey, oh what a run!

The laughter it spreads, infectious and bright,
With seeds that giggle as day turns to night.
A splash of red joy, a wink from the past,
In the echoes of sweetness, laughter holds fast.

Like tickles from friends, it dances and sways,
Filling my heart with hilarious rays.
With each little crunch, I'm lost in the play,
In a world painted red, where jokes come to stay!

So let the good times in bowls overflow,
For every sweet yearning is made for the show.
Let's share in this mirth, while munching on cheer,
With laughter and sweetness, we'll keep it near!

Tales from the Seed Chamber

In chambers dense with ruby seeds,
A party grows, oh what a deed!
With juice that stains and laughter bright,
They dance and juggle through the night.

One seed snorts, the others cheer,
They bounce and roll, it's perfectly clear!
A fruity feud erupts in fun,
All bets are off, the games begun!

A squirt, a splatter, who will win?
The messy melee makes them grin.
They laugh so hard, they nearly burst,
Who knew a seed could quench a thirst?

And as dawn breaks, they settle down,
With sticky smiles, no hint of frown.
In the glowing light, they'll reminisce,
Of wild adventures and fruity bliss.

Sweetness Entangled in Thorns

In a garden, bold and bright,
Sweetness tangled, oh what a sight!
Thorny mismatches, a quirky show,
The fruit's charade steals the glow.

One found romance in a prickly pair,
"Just a kiss, I swear, I dare!"
But ow, oh my! A sharp surprise,
"Next time, more caution," it cries.

A bumblebee, a grand ballet,
Buzzing 'round in sweet dismay.
"Tickle me, oh tangy friend,
Let's spin until this party ends!"

Laughter echoes through the thicket,
A honeyed roar, with puns they picket.
Their tales of sweetness, dark and bright,
Blossom in the morning light.

Elysian Extractions

In a lab of juice, so bizarre,
A scientist dreams of pomegranate spar.
With goggles on, he brews a laugh,
Mixing flavors—what a craft!

"Explosive sweetness!" he yells with glee,
"Guess I'll need an extra degree!"
A splash, a drip, it's fruit on the floor,
"Oh, not again!" he starts to roar.

His assistant trips on a slippery laugh,
A cascade of juice—what a gaffe!
But in the chaos, joy does bloom,
Pink laughter fills the crowded room.

From petals bright, their joy extracted,
In madness sweet, they're so distracted.
With every burst, their spirits rise,
In this fruit lab, joy defies!

The Mosaic Within

In a bowl of bits, they gather round,
Colorful pieces make a joyful sound.
Some red, some pink, a daring hue,
"Oh what fun!" they chirp anew.

One says, "I'll be the cheeky star!"
With juicy antics, they raise the bar.
While another tries to blend with grace,
But smacks a neighbor, a fruity face!

Laughter spills, it spreads like wild,
In this mosaic, they're all beguiled.
Something vibrant, something sweet,
In chaos, their joy finds a beat.

As the bowl wobbles, nobody cares,
They revel in fun, no time for snares.
For within this mix, love does ignite,
A glorious mess, oh what a sight!

A Cup of Forgotten Tales

Once I brewed a fruit-filled tea,
Its color bright, like jubilee.
But every sip, a dance of woe,
The seeds would wiggle, steal the show.

My friends all came for tales to share,
But left with juice in frizzy hair.
With laughter loud, we took a chance,
To wrangle truth in fruity dance.

The pot gave birth to silly schemes,
Of red-stained lips and candy dreams.
We joked of seeds that played all night,
And all our laughs took off in flight.

So raise your cup, let stories flow,
For fruit can lead to quite the show.
In every sip, a tale is spun,
Of silly seeds and fruity fun!

Sweet Intrigues

In gardens lush, where whispers play,
The fruit conspirers plot their way.
A hidden laugh, a juicy plot,
To make us wonder what they've got.

The vibrant hue, it calls to me,
I ponder what the fruit could be.
A game of chance, a taste of fate,
To brave the heart, or simply wait?

With every nibble, smiles ignite,
What's hiding there? A fruity fright?
Or maybe just a burst of fun,
A sticky joke from sun to sun.

So let us gather, share a slice,
Of sweet intrigue, now doesn't that sound nice?
With laughter bright and juice on hands,
We'll weave our tales like fruit-filled bands!

Reflections in Red

A mirror shines, with crimson glow,
My face reflects a juicy show.
I peep and grin, what's on my chin?
A splash of juice, oh where to begin?

The silly seeds start dancing there,
In a fruit-filled world, beyond compare.
With every bite, a giggle grows,
As sticky laughter ebbs and flows.

I wipe my mouth and take a chance,
To join the fruits in joyful dance.
A twirl, a spin, what a delight,
In fruity chaos, hearts take flight.

Let red reflections light the way,
To laughter bright as we all play.
We'll sip and savor, explore and tease,
In fruity wonder, we'll find our ease!

Depths of the Fleshy Core

Within the depths of something sweet,
A fleshy core, a funny feat.
I ventured in, full of surprise,
And found a treasure in disguise.

With squishy bits and seeds galore,
It felt like fun, oh what a score!
Every flick, a juicy mess,
In this wild fruit, we must confess.

A core of laughs, a whisper loud,
It tickled us, we laughed out proud.
From every seed, a story grew,
Of fruitions strange that we all knew.

Dare not to venture with a pout,
In fleshy cores, there's joy throughout.
So lift your spoon, give it a twirl,
And dive right in, let laughter swirl!

Enchantment in a Fragile Sphere

In a garden of blush, I met a red pear,
Rumbled with laughter, casting spells in the air.
"Where's the juice?" it giggled, in fruity delight,
All of its secrets were bursting that night.

With a twist and a turn, it danced on the vine,
Winking at bees, sipping sunshine like wine.
"Do you know the way to a sweet tooth's delight?"
"I'll roll you to candy land, hold on tight!"

A riddle of seeds in each little grin,
Saying, "I'm not a fruit, I'm a party within!"
Whisked away by a breeze, it flew with a cheer,
Claiming, "Eat me! I'm good till the end of the year!"

So here's to the laughter, the whimsy we share,
In a world ripe with giggles, we bounce without care.
Let's crack open the fun, with no worries in sight,
Join the merry parade of this fruity delight!

Lament of the Ripe Harvest

In the glade, fruits moan, nestled round in a row,
Saying, "When ripe, we shine, but we're scared of the blow!"
Sun-kissed and jolly, now wondering the cost,
"What if we're plucked? Oh, what a great loss!"

A cherry piped up, "But think of the pie!
Forget about fate, let's reach for the sky!"
"Or jam!" shouted another, "I'll spread on your toast,
Let's gather our courage, we're loved, after most!"

But in every rich laugh, there's a little despair,
"You know," murmured grape, "there's a chance we can fare.
We'll live on in jar, or as juice we must be,
Even when gone, we're quite the fruit spree!"

So onward they chuckled, through branches so green,
Grappling with fate, laughter was their routine.
"Fear not," said the apricot, "we'll live on the shelf,
For even in jars, we'll be vibrant ourselves!"

Linguistics of Liquid Desire

A swirl in a cup, what language is this?
Each sip tells a tale, oh what fruity bliss!
"I'm more than a drink, can't you see my flair?
I quench for your thirst, and I jiggle with care!"

"Bubbling over, swirling like glee,
My friendship with ice is a wonder to see.
We've every intention to cheer, yes indeed,
Guava and ginger, together we lead!"

Oh what a debate, among liquids so sweet,
"Juice boxes for kids, or does soda compete?"
With carbonation bubbling and zest in the air,
Every drop was now dancing, without any care.

The laughter erupted, and cups soared in flight,
"Let's frolic in flavor, till we dim the night!"
From mixers to sippers, they clinked with zest,
In this vibrant party, they all felt the best!

Verdant Fleeting Moments

In the fields where the green meets the pluck of the sun,
Fruits giggled and jived, saying, "Come have some fun!"
"Life's juicy and sweet, let's make every hour,
A fiesta of flavor in this sunny flower!"

"Dare I be picked? Will someone be brave?"
Challenged the grape, while stuck in a wave.
"I'm rolled by the wind," said the peach with a smile,
"You'll taste my delight; oh, it's totally worthwhile!"

They called out for moments, laughing through leaves,
"Let's play hide and seek, among branches and eaves!"
The fun never faded, each laugh was their mark,
Fleeting yet vibrant, like light through the dark.

So join in this revel, and heed nature's cue,
For all that we harvest brings joy that's so true.
With every sweet bite, and each sip in our hearts,
We dance in these moments, where laughter imparts!

Secrets Encased in Red

Within the ruby shell so bright,
A secret party, oh what a sight!
Each seed a dancer, twirls in time,
In juicy chaos, all is sublime.

But watch your step, they splatter spray,
A sticky prankster's bold display.
With laughter echoing in the air,
Beware the crimson, it's quite a scare!

As laughter bounces 'round the room,
Who knew a fruit could start a bloom?
A pomegranate prank, oh what a tease,
Its juicy mischief aims to please!

So if you seek a funny plight,
Join in the fun, take a bite!
For secrets wrapped in red delight,
Will keep you chuckling through the night.

After the Final Frost

In thawing time at last we meet,
Fluffy coats shed, oh what a feat!
The silly fruits start to emerge,
With giggles rising in the surge.

A frosty farewell, say goodbye,
To snowmen watching all nearby.
The garden's buzzing, quite a show,
As playful seeds begin to grow!

The air is filled with laughter bright,
As fruity friends take early flight.
An orchard full of quirky flair,
With antics sprouting everywhere!

So let us dance beneath the sun,
Our fruit parade has just begun!
For springtime's joy is always sweet,
When laughter and the harvest meet.

Heartstrings and Hibiscus

A heart that's plump and dressed in flair,
Makes quite the case for love and care.
With whimsy woven in its guise,
A fruity giggle, oh how it flies!

Hibiscus blooms stand tall and proud,
While seeds conspire, they're quite the crowd.
Each tiny piece with mischief stored,
An orchestra of laughter roared!

Like tiny fireworks, they burst bright,
Creating chaos in pure delight.
These sweet sensations, oh what a tease,
With every bite, a chuckle frees!

So swing along, let naught remain,
In fruity fun where joy is gained.
With heartstrings strummed in vibrant beats,
A silly melody that repeats.

Secrets of the Autumn Harvest

As autumn leaves begin to fall,
The harvest whispers playful call.
A treasure trove in shades of red,
With laughter buzzing in its spread.

Beneath the branches, secrets hide,
The fruits of joy, a merry ride.
With every bite, a tale to spin,
Of fruity mischief tucked within!

The cider flows, the laughter rolls,
As friends unite and fill their bowls.
A harvest moon with wise old grins,
As nature hosts, the fun begins!

So gather round, let stories flow,
In autumn's grasp, we all shall grow.
For in the red, hilarity lies,
A fruity secret that never dies!

Nectar of Distant Echoes

In a world where fruits wear coats,
A berry giggles and floats.
Juicy tales in every drop,
Sipping sweetness, can't stop!

With seeds that dance like little pals,
Sometimes fierce, like tiny gals.
Bursting laughter, squishy cheer,
Do they whisper in your ear?

Ridiculous dreams within their skin,
They know the secrets held within.
On sunny days, they wave hello,
Wearing hats made of glow!

So, take a bite, don't you dare pause,
For fruity giggles deserve applause!
Trust the laughs that juices bring,
In this carnival of fruit and fling!

Boldness Wrapped in Skin

Courage comes in crimson shells,
With inner gems and silly spells.
Each bite a pop, a zesty cheer,
Boldly swaggering, bring a beer!

You think it's sweet? Oh, just you wait,
It tickles tongues, a fruit on a plate.
Dancing seeds, a daring sight,
A rebel's joy in every bite!

Their skin so smooth, a sassy facade,
But beware the juice, it can be odd!
With each splash, they giggle and scream,
Life's a party, or so it seems!

So grab a spoon, let's dig in deep,
These fruits hold laughter, no need for sleep.
In their boldness, find delight,
Wrapped in skin, a comical bite!

The Taste of Unfulfilled Yearning

Wishing for sweetness, taking a chance,
Biting into promise, but oh, the dance!
Seeds like dreams, scattered wide,
Can't find the nectar where hopes reside.

A sweetened smile turns into a jest,
Life's a fruit that fails the test.
Chasing flavors that don't quite land,
In every core, a silent band.

Yearning for sweetness trapped inside,
Where's my jester, let's take a ride?
A taste of hope with a side of fun,
Yet here I am, still on the run!

But oh, I chuckle, what a delight,
In search of flavors that play out right.
The taste of wanting, wearing a grin,
Life's a comedy, let the fun begin!

Labyrinth of the Fleshy Heart

Inside this maze of juicy walls,
Fruity whispers dance in calls.
Curvy paths of sweetness flow,
Finding routes where laughter grows.

Round and round the seeds do spin,
Chasing dreams that want to win.
Oh, the mischief in each turn,
Lessons found in how we yearn!

Here lies a path of fruity jest,
Tickling taste buds, quite the quest.
With every crunch, a giggle leaps,
In this heart, the laughter keeps.

So wander deep, don't lose your way,
In the fleshy maze, come what may.
For within this fruit, a joyful chart,
Is laughter's echo, the playful heart!

Shadows of the Orchard

In the orchard's giggle and spin,
Fruit secrets hidden within skin.
A squirrel chattered, quite absurd,
Saying, "I'm wiser than the bird!"

With ruby jewels hanging low,
Bumbling bees dance to and fro.
They buzzed about with tiny glee,
"Taste us all—there's plenty of me!"

A breeze tickles cheek and branch,
And all the fruits begin to prance.
"Don't drop me!" cries a cheeky fruit,
"Or I'll bounce hide and go on mute!"

The shadows laugh, the sun's at play,
Orchard antics claim the day.
In nature's jest, we all partake,
For every fruit has jokes to make.

Echoes of a Forbidden Feast

A banquet laid under a tree,
But what's that? A new decree!
"No feasting here, it can't be done!"
Yelled a pear at the cheek of the sun.

Ripe grapes giggle, roll and sway,
"Let's sneak a bite—it's our parade!"
They whispered sweetly, laughing loud,
As if they defied fate, proud.

A melon winked, with a sly grin,
"Let the munching games begin!"
But oranges frowned, wanting peace,
"Let's share our wealth—we're all a feast!"

Echoes carried on the breeze,
Of fruity battles and playful tease.
In this orchard, joy is key,
Forbidden? Only when you're free!

Heartbeats of the Orchard

Underneath the leafy shade,
Fruits have hearts that laugh and fade.
A rambunctious berry shouts,
"Who needs a crown when you've got clouts?"

A watermelon thumped—what a sound!
"I'm king here! Look at me, round!"
The apples snickered, rolled their eyes,
"His royal demeanor's full of lies!"

A joyful dance swept through the air,
As hearts of fruit began to share.
"Let's beat together, make a tune!"
Bellowed cherries, over the moon.

In this garden, silliness reigned,
No serious thoughts were ever retained.
Heartbeat echoes weave and twine,
In this place, laughter's divine!

The Siren's Scarlet Call

A siren's voice from vines did sing,
"Join the fun, oh, come and swing!"
Red fruits giggled, swaying free,
As if they danced in playful glee.

"Beware the pull, do not be lost!"
Cried the fig, weighing the cost.
"But what's the risk of tasting fun?"
Laughed the grape, "Let's all just run!"

With laughter bright as a summer's day,
The vine's sweet charm led us away.
To secrets hidden in leaves and cheer,
We feasted lightly, year after year.

So heed the call of the playful breeze,
For in this dance, we find our keys.
A siren's laugh, so sweet, so bright,
In scarlet hues, we take our flight.

Remnants of Ancient Myths

In the garden where legends peek,
A fruit with secrets starts to speak.
"I'm juicy and bright, but don't get too close,
My seeds hold tales of a billion ghost!"

Old gods must chuckle from heights above,
As I juggle my seeds with comical love.
"O Hermes, pour me another round,
These tales are sweet, but they bounce off the ground!"

So myths get tangled in vines of cheer,
As squirrels debate which fruit to steer.
With each bite, laughter fills the air,
Ancient humor, if you dare to share!

In the end, if you find seeds in your hair,
Just know that the stories will always be there.
A snack for the mind, a feast for the soul,
Let's all raise a glass and play our role!

A Orchard's Lament

In the orchard, the laughter bred,
The fruits plot jokes while I'm misled.
"Hey buddy, I'm red, but why so sour?
Just wait and see, I'll bright up your hour!"

The wind carries whispers from branch to branch,
"Hey, do you hear the apple's last dance?"
"Sure do! He's spinning with quite the flair,
While I just sit here, avoiding despair!"

The pears roll their eyes at the grapevine's talk,
"Let's set this rumor on a nice long walk!"
With no legs to run, it's all in the jest,
I guess in the orchard, we love to jest!

As sun pours in laughter through leafy cheeks,
Dance with us, won't you? A picnic of freaks!
Crunchy friendships are born in this space,
Just watch your step and enjoy your place.

Divided by Nature's Design

In a world of green, oh what a mess,
I'm stuck with my pals, each one a stress.
"You look too fine, let's peel back your skin!
Your outer shell hides the chaos within!"

Each seed has a grudge, each fruit a plot,
"I'm the star here!" says the forgotten shot.
As branches collide in a comic dance,
I'm just waiting for my chance to prance!

Sunlight streams in like a bad stand-up joke,
While bees buzz around, as chaos they stoke.
"I swear I saw this apple in a gown,
But all I got's a beet, wearing a crown!"

The harvest looms nearer, we're all in a row,
Awaiting our fate with a comical glow.
So let's toast to the fruits and their vibrant show,
In nature's wild theater, we steal the show!

Sips of Eternity

Under the sun, we gather and scheme,
With sips of sweetness, we dream and beam.
"Raise your cups high, let's toast to the stars,
Where juice flows like laughter, banishing scars!"

In this quirky crowd of juicy delight,
A fig plays the lute, what a comical sight!
"Let's sip on tomorrow with yesterday's cheer,
If I'm stuffed with seeds, then who's your dear?"

To quench our thirst, we dance and we laugh,
Creating chaos in nature's great path.
"If life gives you juice, just sip it with zest,
And ponder the fruits that you loved the best!"

As tummies rumble and giggles arise,
In this playful feast under blue skies.
A gathering of flavor, forever we stay,
In sips of eternity, we sip and sway!

Beneath the Fleshy Veil

In a garden where secrets grow,
A silly fruit with a juicy glow.
Witty seeds all packed tight,
In a burst of laughs, they take flight.

Peel back the skin, oh what a mess,
Sticky fingers, no time to impress.
With every bite, a giggle ensues,
A fruity riddle, we just can't refuse.

Who knew such laughter could bleed from a skin?
Delicious chaos where fun begins.
Grape envy? No, we're not that fond,
This silly fruit's our grand response!

So come and join the fruity jest,
In a world of laughter, we're truly blessed.
With every crunch, let the giggles start,
For joy is found in this fleshy heart.

Nectar of Life's Duality

Juicy jewels, oh what a sight,
A cheeky fruit that takes a bite.
With every taste, a playful cheer,
A sweet surprise that brings us near.

Dancing with seeds like tiny stars,
Tickling tongues from near and far.
Who knew that life could seem so funny?
When you've got sweetness, honey's just runny!

A punch of tart, a dash of sweet,
In every squirt, there's joy to greet.
I've heard a whisper, I think it's true,
This silly fruit's a love rendezvous!

So raise a glass and laugh aloud,
For life's a party, wear it proud.
With every drop from playful lips,
We toast to joy with fruity sips!

Bounty of the Blossom

In a swaying tree, a bloom's delight,
Where fruits like laughter take their flight.
Silly seeds all snug inside,
Whispers of joy they cannot hide.

Harvesting giggles, plucking cheer,
Every bite brings friends near.
In the orchard, feelings swell,
As we bite into this fruity spell.

Juicy laughter rolls off the tongue,
In this party, we're forever young.
Even squirrels can't help but dance,
As they munch and take a chance!

So gather 'round and crack a grin,
For the bounty's ripe, let fun begin.
From blossom to fruit, a silly spree,
In the garden of laughter, we're always free!

The Hidden Temptation

What secrets hide behind this skin?
A cheeky grin, let's dig right in!
With every pop, a splash of glee,
In this fruity rapture, we're all carefree.

A playful heist from nature's vault,
A daring bite, oh, what a jolt!
Violet seeds, a ticklish dance,
Just one nibble puts you in a trance.

Covered in laughter, bursting with fun,
Who knew this fruit could be so pun?
In sticky joy, we find our spark,
A sweetness in laughter leaves its mark.

Let's raise our hands to fruity cheer,
With every crunch, our hearts will clear.
So come join me and take a part,
In this adventure of a hidden heart!

Crimson Seeds of Longing

In a garden of fruits, so bold and round,
A juicy tale of seeds is found.
With laughter echoing through the trees,
I tripped on a vine, oh, how it teased!

Red drops fell, like kisses thrown,
While squirrels danced, their mischief shown.
I tried to barter, a seed for a snack,
But that cheeky bird just laughed and flew back!

A juicy explosion, surprising and bright,
Sticky fingers in the warm daylight.
In a battle of wits, I plead my case,
But those seeds just giggled, in a fruity embrace!

Transfixed by a fruit, a comedic ride,
Each bite a riddle, full of pride.
With a wink and a laugh, I stroll along,
Singing with joy, my sweet, silly song.

Whispers of Juicy Secrets

In the shade of the fig, secrets do dance,
Whispers of fruit, a mischievous chance.
I swear I heard a seed softly sigh,
And a wink from the grapes, oh my, oh my!

Beneath leaves so green, tales unfold,
Of a berry that dared to be daringly bold.
I laugh at the stories those cherries could tell,
Of juicy love notes, and mishaps as well!

With a squish and a splash, fruit tales collide,
Their giggles erupting, can't run or hide.
I chased after lemons, they rolled down the lane,
With laughter and juice, delightful and plain!

Berry much fun, as I twirl in delight,
With every bite, a new added light.
In the orchard's embrace, a whimsical jest,
Where fruits spin tales, and secrets are dressed.

Blood-Bound Desires

In a patch of red fruit, desires do bloom,
Sweet and succulent, they chase away gloom.
I reached for a berry, so bright and divine,
But slipped on the juice, oh, what a line!

With a pop and a squish, the juice flew high,
And laughter erupted, oh my, oh my!
Those seeds have a way of making me grin,
As I tumble and roll, letting the fun in.

Crimson vows whispered in every soft bite,
Yet sticky fingers only brought on delight.
A wobbly fruit dance, on this merry spree,
Where love and laughter get tangled with glee!

So here with my bounty, I sip and I share,
In this garden of dreams, joy fills the air.
With each juicy tease and giggle that flies,
I'm blood-bound to bliss, under berry skies.

Fruit of Forgotten Love

In a basket of fruit, memories lay bare,
Tales of sweet kisses floating in air.
Oh, the grapes that I loved, now jelly on toast,
In a jar of old stories, they laugh the most!

Cherry on top of my glorious misfit,
Its tales of love skewed into pure wit.
While apples roll by, with a wink and a cheer,
Old forgotten romances, still making us leer!

Banana peels whisper of mishaps in flair,
With every slip, a giggle to share.
My heart's tangled up in this fruity old joke,
Where the sour and sweet dance, with love as their yoke!

So here's to the fruit and the joy they impart,
In laughter we find, it's a beautiful art.
Amidst fruity treasures, both quirky and bright,
I cherish these moments, sweet laughter's delight.

Juicy Echoes of the Past

In gardens where secrets reside,
Bouncing seeds on a thrilling ride.
They giggle and bounce, can't hold a seat,
Whispering tales of the summer's heat.

A plump fruit dared to wear a crown,
While slipping on juice, it slid right down.
Laughter erupted, they danced in glee,
Beneath the shade of an old fig tree.

Memories stain the picnic cloth,
With juice that dares, none can be wroth.
Crimson splashes tell tales of yore,
As laughter echoes, they want even more.

So gather round, let the fun begin,
With sticky fingers, laughter's the win.
For all those tales hidden in red,
Are sillier now, that's what they said!

The Fruit's Hidden Quest

In the land of snacks, a quest untold,
A fruity mission, brave and bold.
To find the crunch, to seek the sweet,
A round adventure, oh what a treat!

With a caper, they rolled and bounced,
Chasing each other, imagination pronounced.
In dazzling colors, they'd flash and flirt,
Cackling and giggling, it all felt like dirt.

In search of a throne, they stumbled and fell,
Juicy mischief, they know all too well.
Pits were flying, laughter's grand race,
As they claimed their glory, a juicy embrace.

With laughter still ringing, they conquered the day,
A fruit brigade! Hip hip hooray!
So juice up, friends, let your spirit swell,
In this fruity escapade, we'll always excel!

A Sweet Redemption

From the depths of the bowl, a treasure shines,
With sugary secrets and fruity designs.
Plucked from the tree, it's seen it all,
In kitchens and picnics, it answers the call.

A wink from the seeds, a cheeky grin,
As they plot and plan to steal a win.
They hid in the fridge, like little spies,
Plotting their heist under fizzy skies.

With a slurp and a squint, they knock on wood,
To find the sweet treasure, oh how good!
Crimson delight in a jumbled heap,
Turns out redemption is a fruity leap.

In laughter and sweetness, they find their way,
To celebrate life in a sticky ballet.
So, gather around for a zesty embrace,
As seeds burst with joy, oh what a place!

Radiance Within the Rind

Beneath the surface, a party resides,
With zest and giggles, they dance and glide.
Rind wrapped tight, like a fruit in glee,
They burst forth laughing, wild and free.

A vibrant squad in a cheeky fest,
Competing for giggles, they give it their best.
Berry brothers, citrus cousins, and more,
A fruity shindig, oh what a score!

With laughter like bubbles, they pop and cheer,
Bringing together the friends far and near.
In every bite, the joy overflows,
Radiance unleashed from where nobody knows.

So crack open joy, let the flavors collide,
In every sweet moment, let laughter abide.
For deep in the rind, there's much to find,
A zestful reminder of life's joyful grind!

Bounty and Belonging in Red Form.

In a garden full of glee,
A fruit of joy swings free,
Giggling seeds, no shame to share,
All together, without a care.

A mischief-maker's delight,
Dancing 'neath the moonlight,
Juicy laughter spills around,
In this fruit, fun is found.

With a burst, the juices fly,
Little raindrops in the sky,
Nature's prankster, full of jest,
In this bounty, we are blessed.

So grab a knife, let's have some fun,
Slice it open, now we run!
A fruit so bold, with quirky charms,
In its sweetness, please disarm.

Crimson Secrets

Whispers hide within each fold,
As secrets in red silk are told,
A curious crunch calls my name,
With each bite, more laughter came.

Little seeds, like spies they sit,
Giggling softly, not a wit,
In the bowl, they play their roles,
Crimson secrets on their strolls.

What's in here? A prank so grand,
Juicy chaos at our hand,
With every taste, a jolly cheer,
Bursting bubbles of fruity beer!

Around the table, tales unfurl,
As laughter spins and twirls,
With this fruit, the smiles are rife,
In every bite, we find good life!

Seeds of Desire

In the bowl, bright seeds do gleam,
Each one's a funky little dream,
Their promise laughs from deep within,
A taste so fine, where to begin?

Jests and giggles, in each pop,
Watch them bounce, and never stop,
Fruity shenanigans in the air,
With every nibble, joy we share.

Unexpected sourness meets the sweet,
A prankster feast, oh what a treat!
Each seed a little trickster's game,
Fueling our fun, unashamed!

In this playful banquet, we unite,
Laughter erupts, oh what a sight!
Seeds of desire cruising free,
Taste buds dancing, wild and carefree!

Beneath the Ruby Skin

Beneath the skin, a party swells,
A ruby realm where laughter dwells,
Open it up, let the fun commence,
Juicy joy makes perfect sense.

Each slice a giggle, each seed a rhyme,
Tickling taste buds every time,
Dare to dive into this delight,
In each burst, there's sheer light!

With ruby chaos, don't be shy,
Relish every playful pie,
Sticky fingers, laughter loud,
In this fruit, we are all proud.

So grab your friends, let's have a feast,
With this cheeky fruit, joy increased,
In every nibble, let's confide,
The treasures of laughter, our joy inside!

Chosen by the Harvest Moon

In the orchard where the moon hangs tight,
Fruits in costume, a comical sight.
Shadows dance, a giggle or two,
As the squirrels conspire, planning their stew.

A fruit flops over, with a juicy quake,
"Is it dinner? Or just a big mistake?"
The chickens cluck, wearing shades of red,
Hatching schemes from their cozy bed.

At midnight's hour, laughter erupts,
While curious rabbits cheer as they sup.
The harvest shines with a playful glow,
As nature's revelry begins to flow.

Under the moon, the mischief thrives,
Even the crickets dance and high-fives.
So gather 'round, as laughter does bloom,
In the patch of joy 'neath the harvest moon.

The Crucible of Desire

In the garden of wishes, they try to impress,
All the fruits wear outfits, a fabulous mess.
With a wink and a twist, they flirt and they bray,
Plotting a picnic, come what may!

One cheeky berry shouts, "I'm the best treat!"
While the apples roll their eyes in defeat.
Beneath the bright sun, they gossip and scheme,
Each one a player in this fruity dream.

The bananas slide in with a slippery grin,
Challenging oranges, "Let the games begin!"
A race to the basket, they try to compete,
But the cherries just joke, "Is it snack time or feat?"

As desires overflow in this salad of glee,
Who will reign champion? Just wait and see!
With a splash and a crunch, the fun never tires,
In the garden's great tale of whimsical fires.

Enigmas Within the Shell

Beneath a thick armor, the secrets reside,
Much like a magician with tricks tucked inside.
The nuts whisper tales of bravery bold,
Riddles and puns, their stories unfold.

"Why was the walnut so late for the show?"
It cracked up the crowd, shouting, "I didn't know!"
The almonds chipped in, with a jocular flair,
"I thought it was nutty to just sit and stare!"

In the shell of a mystery, drama's afoot,
As the peanuts play tag on their cozy wood.
Dancing and laughing, they twist and they roll,
With jokes and jests, they capture the whole.

So gather 'round, for the shells hold delight,
In a festival of flavor, from day into night.
Each one unique, with tales of the wild,
Join in the laughter, like a curious child.

Unraveled Threads of Color

Stringing together a patchwork of cheer,
Fruits flaunt their colors, oh so clear!
Tangerine twirls with a ruby-red sway,
Beguiled by the laughter that blooms in the fray.

"What's the best riddle?" a grape sings aloud,
"Why did the apple not join the crowd?"
Peeling back layers, the audience roars,
As the melon joins in, with laughs that just pours.

Each fruity thread weaves a tale of delight,
Painting the banquet that sparkles so bright.
With giggles aplenty, they spin in a dance,
Creating a fiesta, a colorful chance.

So gather your friends, don your silliest hat,
In this fruity bazaar, where none will fall flat.
Unraveled in laughter, we savor the fun,
Threads of connection, as bright as the sun.

www.ingramcontent.com/pod-product-compliance
Lightning Source LLC
Chambersburg PA
CBHW060138230426
43661CB00003B/470